THE BEAT
6 STUDIES FOR G

JOY IN SUFFERING

Receiving Your Reward

David Lambert

ZondervanPublishingHouse
Grand Rapids, Michigan

A Division of HarperCollins*Publishers*

Requests for information should be addressed to:
Zondervan Publishing House
Grand Rapids, MI 49530

ISBN 0-310-59673-4

Edited by Jack Kuhatschek
Cover design by John M. Lucas
Cover photograph by Kaz Mori
Interior design by Louise Bauer

Printed in the United States of America

93 94 95 96 97 98 / ❖ DP / 10 9 8 7 6 5 4 3 2 1

Contents

The Beatitude Series   5

Introducing Joy in Suffering   11

1. STANDING STRONG   15
    Daniel 3:8 – 27; Job 1

2. OBEYING GOD RATHER THAN MAN   20
    Acts 5:12 – 42

3. SUFFERING AS A CHRISTIAN   26
    1 Peter 1:6 – 7; 2:19 – 23; 4:12 – 19

4. RESPONDING TO YOUR ENEMIES   31
    Luke 6:27 – 36; Romans 12:14 – 21

5. FIXING YOUR EYES ON JESUS   37
    Hebrews 12:1 – 12

6. RECEIVING YOUR REWARD   42
    Matthew 5:10 – 12; Luke 6:22 – 23, 26

Leader's Notes   47

The Beatitude Series

Welcome to the Beatitude Series. This series is designed to help you develop the eight character qualities found in those whom Jesus calls "blessed."

The Beatitudes are among the best-known and best-loved words of Jesus. They form the heart of the Sermon on the Mount, found in Matthew 5–7 and Luke 6:17–49. In eight brief statements Jesus describes the lifestyle that God desires and rewards:

> *Blessed are the poor in spirit,*
> *for theirs is the kingdom of heaven.*
> *Blessed are those who mourn,*
> *for they will be comforted.*
> *Blessed are the meek,*
> *for they will inherit the earth.*

Blessed are those who hunger and thirst for righteousness,
   for they will be filled.
Blessed are the merciful,
   for they will be shown mercy.
Blessed are the pure in heart,
   for they will see God.
Blessed are the peacemakers,
   for they will be called sons of God.
Blessed are those who are persecuted because of righteousness,
   for theirs is the kingdom of heaven.

The Beatitudes turn the world's values upside down. We are tempted to say: "*Wretched* are the poor, for they have so little money. *Wretched* are those who mourn, for no one will hear their cries. *Wretched* are the meek, for they will be trampled by the powerful." Yet Jesus shatters our stereotypes and asserts that the poor will be rich, the mourners will be comforted, and the meek will inherit everything. What a strange kingdom he offers!

In recent years there has been some confusion about the kind of blessing Christ promises in these verses. The Beatitudes have been described as "God's prescription for happiness." One book has even called them "The Be-Happy Attitudes."

The Greek word *makarios* can mean "happy." J. B. Phillips translates the opening words of each beatitude, "How happy are . . . !" Nevertheless, John Stott writes:

> It is seriously misleading to render *makarios* "happy." For happiness is a subjective state, whereas Jesus is making an objective judgment about these people. He is declaring not what they may feel like ("happy"), but what God thinks of them and what on that account they are: they are "blessed."[1]

The eight guides in the Beatitude Series give you an in-depth look at each beatitude. But Jesus is not describing eight different types of people—some who are meek, others who are merciful, and still others who are peacemakers. He desires to see all eight character qualities in every one of his followers.

That's a tall order! Only those who enter Christ's kingdom by faith can expect such a transformation. And only those who serve the King can enjoy his rewards.

Our prayer is that The Beatitude Series will give you a clearer and deeper grasp of what it truly means to be blessed.

HOW TO USE THE BEATITUDE SERIES

The Beatitude Series is designed to be flexible. You can use the guides in any order that is best for you or your group. They are ideal for Sunday-school classes, small groups, one-on-one relationships, or as materials for your quiet times.

Because each guide contains only six studies, you can easily explore more than one beatitude. In a Sunday-school class, any two guides can be combined for a quarter (twelve weeks), or the entire series can be covered in a year.

Each study deliberately focuses on a limited number of passages, usually only one or two. That allows you to see each passage in its context, avoiding the temptation of prooftexting and the frustration of "Bible hopscotch" (jumping from verse to verse). If you would like to look up additional passages, a Bible concordance will give the most help.

The Beatitude Series helps you *discover* what the Bible says rather than simply *telling* you the answers. The questions encourage you to think and to explore options rather than merely to fill in the blanks with one-word answers.

Leader's notes are provided in the back of each guide. They show how to lead a group discussion, provide additional information on questions, and suggest ways to deal with problems that may come up in the discussion. With such helps,

7

someone with little or no experience can lead an effective study.

SUGGESTIONS FOR INDIVIDUAL STUDY

1. Begin each study with prayer. Ask God to help you understand the passage and to apply it to your life.

2. A good modern translation, such as the *New International Version,* the *New American Standard Bible,* or the *New Revised Standard Version,* will give you the most help. Questions in this guide, however, are based on the *New International Version.*

3. Read and reread the passage(s). You must know what the passage says before you can understand what it means and how it applies to you.

4. Write your answers in the space provided in the study guide. This will help you to clearly express your understanding of the passage.

5. Keep a Bible dictionary handy. Use it to look up any unfamiliar words, names, or places.

SUGGESTIONS FOR GROUP STUDY

1. Come to the study prepared. Careful preparation will greatly enrich your time in group discussion.

2. Be willing to join in the discussion. The leader of the group will not be lecturing but will encourage people to discuss what they have learned in the passage. Plan to share what God has taught you in your individual study.

3. Stick to the passage being studied. Base your answers on the verses being discussed rather than on outside authorities such as commentaries or your favorite author or speaker.

4. Try to be sensitive to the other members of the group. Listen attentively when they speak, and be affirming when-

ever you can. This will encourage more hesitant members of the group to participate.

5. Be careful not to dominate the discussion. By all means participate! But allow others to have equal time.

6. If you are the discussion leader, you will find additional suggestions and helpful ideas in the leader's notes at the back of the guide.

Note

1. *The Message of the Sermon on the Mount* (Downers Grove, Ill.: InterVarsity Press, 1978), p. 33.

Introducing
Joy in Suffering

> *Blessed are those who are persecuted because of righteousness,*
> *for theirs is the kingdom of heaven.*

On April 8, 1945, Lutheran pastor Dietrich Bonhoeffer led a short worship service in the Gestapo prison at Flossenburg, Germany. He brought a short message and had just finished his final prayer when two guards entered and said, "Prisoner Bonhoeffer, come with us." All present knew the meaning of those words. He said his final good-byes, adding, "This is the end, but for me it is the beginning of life."[1]

The next day, April 9, 1945, Dietrich Bonhoeffer was hanged by the direct order of Heinrich Himmler because of his staunch resistance, as a matter of Christian conscience, to the Nazi regime.

The text for his message in that final worship service was Isaiah 53:5, "By his wounds we are healed." And the words he wrote not long before his death echo after him:

> Suffering, then, is the badge of true discipleship. The disci-
> ple is not above his master. Following Christ means *passio*
> *passiva,* suffering because we have to suffer. That is why
> Luther reckoned suffering among the marks of the true

church, and one of the memoranda drawn up in preparation for the Augsburg Confession similarly defines the Church as the community of those "who are persecuted and martyred for the gospel's sake" . . . Discipleship means allegiance to the suffering Christ, and it is therefore not at all surprising that Christians should be called upon to suffer. In fact, it is a joy and a token of his grace.[2]

Dietrich Bonhoeffer was not the first Christian to suffer for his beliefs. Stephen became the first Christian martyr when, after his no-holds-barred, in-your-face message to the Sanhedrin in Acts 7, he was stoned to death. Church tradition has it that only John, of all the apostles, escaped a violent death. Others were hanged, crucified, stoned, stabbed with swords and spears, and killed in a variety of other ways.

From Nero's callous, bloody, politically motivated vendetta against Christians to the enforced intolerance of the Middle Ages (enforced, usually, by burning at the stake), to the bitter resistance encountered by the first modern missionaries in the nineteenth century, to the modern-day struggles of such oppressed Christians as Samuel Lamb in China—whose repeated and lengthy imprisonments for preaching the gospel have not deterred him from what God has called him to do—Christians have seldom escaped suffering of one kind or another. Bonhoeffer's words were simply an accurate backward look at centuries of pain, oppression, insult, and bloodshed.

Jesus warned us: "If the world hates you, keep in mind that it hated me first. . . . You do not belong to the world, but I have chosen you out of the world. That is why the world hates you. . . . If they persecuted me, they will persecute you also" (John 15:18–20). And history, recent as well as ancient, has proven his words. As John Stott points out in *The Message of the Sermon on the Mount:*

> However hard we may try to make peace with some people, they refuse to live at peace with us. Not all attempts at reconciliation succeed. Indeed, some take the initiative to

oppose us, and in particular to "revile" or slander us. This is not because of our foibles or idiosyncrasies, but "for righteousness' sake" (10) and "on my account" (11), that is, because they find distasteful the righteousness for which we hunger and thirst (6), and because they have rejected the Christ we seek to follow. Persecution is simply the clash between irreconcilable value-systems.[3]

Persecution is not unique to Christianity. The Jews have been subject to untold suffering over the centuries, including World War II's Holocaust, and surely the American Indians were persecuted by cavalry and settler alike in the nineteenth century. Persecution along racial or cultural or social lines has been rampant throughout history. But the Christian's prescribed response to persecution is truly unique. Only those of us who follow Christ are entreated to love and bless and pray for our persecutors; only we are told to "rejoice and be glad" in our sufferings (Matt. 5:12).

Why are we asked to do something so unnatural? Why can't we simply lament our sufferings and call down God's wrath on our persecutors, as David the psalmist did? How are we to overcome our instincts for revenge and anger and self-preservation?

We know that what God requires of us he also empowers us to do. So let us investigate, in this study of the final beatitude, God's instructions to us regarding suffering for Christ—so that we will be able to rejoice in it when it comes.

David Lambert

Notes

1. John W. Doberstein, Introduction to *Life Together* by Dietrich Bonhoeffer (San Francisco: Harper & Row, 1954), p. 13.
2. *The Message of the Sermon on the Mount,* p. 53.
3. Ibid, p. 52.

1

Standing Strong

DANIEL 3:8–27; JOB 1

We thrilled, as children, to the stories of the suffering saints, Old Testament and New: the stoning of Stephen, Daniel among the lions, Paul imprisoned—and Shadrach, Meshach, and Abednego thrown into the flames. But unlike the brightly colored pieces of paper our teachers placed on the flannelgraph, the flames those three young men were thrown into were real. And seven times hotter than usual.

And although they would come out of it in fine shape, they didn't know that going in.

Suffering is real for most of us now, too, in ways that we never dreamed of as children. And because of that, those old stories have new meaning.

In this study we will look at four people who underwent great suffering to see how they bore up under it.

1. Which Christian martyrs, or other Christians who have suffered for their beliefs—biblical, historical, or contemporary—have been inspiring to you?

Why are those particular people inspiring?

2. Read Daniel 3:8–27. Why do you think the astrologers incite King Nebuchadnezzar against Shadrach, Meshach, and Abednego (vv. 8–12)?

3. Although Nebuchadnezzar is furious, he is still willing to give the three Jews another chance (v. 15). How would you describe their attitudes and manner as they reply to Nebuchadnezzar (vv. 16–18)?

4. How does their reply differ from what you might expect from:

   ❑ a warrior?

   ❑ a diplomat?

   ❑ a coward?

5. How would the meaning of the story have changed if the outcome had been different—if God had chosen not to rescue the three Jews but rather to allow them to be martyred for their faith?

6. In what parts of the world today are Christians arrested, tortured, or subjected to other forms of persecution for reasons similar to those of Shadrach, Meshach, and Abednego?

7. Read Job 1. How does the author go out of his way to show that Job does not deserve to suffer (vv. 1–5)?

8. How do you feel about the fact that you may be just as vulnerable to suffering as those who don't serve God?

9. In verses 9–11, what picture does Satan give of Job's righteousness?

10. How does wave after wave of hardship hit Job during a single day (vv. 13–19)?

11. How do you think you would respond to a series of calamities of that magnitude in that space of time?

12. What is remarkable about Job's attitude in verses 20–22?

13. How does Job's attitude compare with that of Shadrach, Meshach, and Abednego in Daniel 3:16–18?

14. In what ways can the examples of Shadrach, Meshach, Abednego, and Job help us deal with persecution and hardship?

MEMORY VERSE

> *"Naked I came from my mother's womb,*
> *and naked I will depart.*
> *The Lord gave and the Lord has taken away;*
> *may the name of the Lord be praised."*

Job 1:21

BETWEEN STUDIES

This week, identify those areas in which you are most vulnerable to the fear of being opposed or rejected because of your faith in Christ. In which areas would you find it most difficult to stand strong, like Shadrach, Meshach, and Abednego, or to wait patiently, like Job?

Would your pride be damaged by insult, shunning, or contempt? Do you shrink from physical pain? Do you cling to your possessions? Would their loss cause you great emotional distress?

Take a personal inventory of your vulnerability to opposition and rejection, and then pray for greater strength to stand firm in every area of your life.

FOR FURTHER STUDY

Read the following passages describing other incidences of persecution:

❑ Daniel 6

❑ Matthew 26:47–27:50

❑ Acts 5:17–42; 6:8–7:60; 9:19–30; 23:12–32

What can we learn from these examples?

2

Obeying God Rather than Man

ACTS 5:12–42

In the 1780s, a young, impoverished British cobbler and lay minister named William Carey developed a revolutionary belief: that the primary mission of the church was spreading the gospel to the unchurched.

> Many, if not most, eighteenth-century churchmen believed that the Great Commission was given only to the apostles, and therefore converting the "heathen" was no concern of theirs, especially if it were not tied to colonialism. When Carey presented his ideas to a group of ministers, one of them retorted: "Young man, sit down. When God pleases to convert the heathen, He will do it without your aid or mine."[1]

Carey did not sit down. In the years to follow, he wrote a ground-breaking book on the importance of missions, inspired the formation of a new mission society, and became one of the first modern missionaries to be sent overseas (to India).

The criticism continued. His own father denounced him as mad. His wife criticized his every decision. At one point his mission board became so critical of his methods that he was forced to withdraw for a short time. But Carey persevered, and in the end won a reputation as "the Father of Modern Missions."

All because William Carey decided to obey God rather than man.

1. Can you think of any historical or contemporary figures who were punished because they sought to obey God?

2. Read Acts 5:12–42. Why are the high priest and his associates so filled with jealousy that they throw Peter and the rest of the apostles in jail (v. 18)?

3. After an angel of the Lord frees the apostles, they go back to the temple courts (vv. 19–20). What conclusion can you draw from the fact that they do not flee for their own safety?

4. Why do you suppose the temple guards are afraid that the people might react violently if they use force against the apostles (v. 26)?

Why might the people have been on the side of the apostles?

5. In addition to jealousy, what reasons might the high priest and the Sanhedrin have had for hating and persecuting the apostles (vv. 27–28; compare with Matt. 27:25)?

For what similar reasons might non-Christians persecute Christians today?

6. Peter states the crux of the issue in verse 29: "We must obey God rather than men." Although that sounds perfectly logical, why are we often tempted to give in to peer pressure?

7. How did the apostles know that they were indeed doing what God wanted them to do (see vv. 18–20)?

8. Since few of us receive direct messages from God today, how can we know what God wants us to do so that we can obey him with confidence?

9. How does God protect the apostles from serious harm in this particular case (vv. 33–40)?

Will God always protect us from harm if we obey him? Explain.

10. Although the flogging the apostles received must have been painful, what is their response (vv. 40–42)?

11. What are some ways we might obey God rather than man in our own day?

What are some of the possible consequences?

MEMORY VERSE

The apostles left the Sanhedrin, rejoicing because they had been counted worthy of suffering disgrace for the Name.

Acts 5:41

BETWEEN STUDIES

Spend some time this week reviewing the decisions you've made in life. Were there times when you could say, "I obeyed God rather than man"? Do you recall times when you chose against God's apparent will because of the insistence of other people (including parents) or because you feared that others would ridicule or pity you? Ask God's forgiveness for those times.

Evaluate carefully the decisions you make this week. Are there situations in which you will be tempted to compromise because of peer pressure? Pray for God's help to stand firm.

FOR FURTHER STUDY

Sadly, when we obey people rather than God, it's often out of fear—we fear the consequences of disappointing or angering our peers more than we fear the consequences of disobeying God.

We have forgotten the biblical concept of "fear" of the Lord. Examine the following verses:

- ❏ Exodus 1:15–21
- ❏ 2 Samuel 22:7–20
- ❏ 2 Kings 17:36–39
- ❏ Job 40:1–14; 41:11
- ❏ Psalms 25:12–14; 103:11, 13, 17
- ❏ Proverbs 16:6
- ❏ Matthew 10:28
- ❏ Hebrews 12:28–29

What principles can you extract from these verses that could directly affect your decision-making?

Note

1. Ruth A. Tucker, *From Jerusalem to Irian Jaya* (Grand Rapids, Mich.: Zondervan Publishing House, 1983), p. 115.

3

Suffering as a Christian

1 PETER 1:6–7; 2:19–23; 4:12–19

- Martyr complex
- Masochistic
- Very low self-image
- Neurotic
- Self-destructive and suicidal

Modern psychology gives us many terms for those who willingly submit to suffering or persecution. When I hear those terms, I think of a friend of mine who became convinced in Bible college that God had called him to a life of difficult, dangerous service. To prepare himself to withstand pain, he always had his dental work done without Novocaine.

Ouch.

Going a little overboard? Maybe. But there's no escaping the fact that the Bible does not always talk about suffering as something to be avoided. In fact, suffering is often talked about in positive terms—as a privilege.

Not a pleasant thought. But in this study we'll examine some of those passages in order to better understand the place suffering has in our lives.

1. Many of the tenets of Christianity seem foolish to those who don't believe them. What teachings of Christianity make no sense to people in our modern world?

2. Read 1 Peter 1:6–7. What do you suppose Peter means when he says that for a "little while" we may experience grief through our trials? How long is a "little while"?

3. Although the purposes of suffering are many and complex, what are some of the purposes suggested in verse 7?

4. Read 1 Peter 2:19–23. Think of a time you were punished or disciplined for something you had done wrong. How did you feel about it?

5. Think of a time you were punished or disciplined unjustly, when you had done nothing wrong. How did you feel about that?

Why is this kind of suffering spoken of as "commendable before God" (v. 20)?

6. Verse 21 begins, "To this you were called . . ." Define "this" in your own words—to *what* were you called?

7. What advice might sensible, practical, modern people have given Jesus if they found out he was about to be arrested unjustly and subjected to the indignities spoken of in verses 21–23?

8. Christ "entrusted himself to him who judges justly" (v. 23). How can we do the same, and what will it mean in our lives?

9. Read 1 Peter 4:12–19. What does Peter suggest about the place of suffering in the Christian's life (v. 12)?

10. Peter tells us to rejoice that we can "participate in the sufferings of Christ" (v. 13). What does it mean to participate in Christ's sufferings? (See also Philippians 3:7–11.)

11. What are some of the ways we might be "insulted because of the name of Christ" (v. 14)?

12. According to Peter, why can we rejoice when we suffer for Christ (vv. 13–14, 16; see also 1:7)?

13. Based on the information in these passages in 1 Peter, what conclusions can you draw about the meaning of "suffering as a Christian"?

MEMORY VERSES

If you suffer for doing good and you endure it, this is commendable before God. To this you were called, because Christ suffered for you, leaving you an example, that you should follow in his steps.

1 Peter 2:20–21

BETWEEN STUDIES

Keep track this week of the unpleasant experiences: arguments, insults, physical pain, slights, frustrations, disappointments. Each time you experience something you would rather not, review the answers you came up with to questions 11 and 12.

How does your suffering this week fit in with your answers to those questions? Are you suffering for Christ? Are you suffering unjustly? Or is your suffering simply a natural consequence of a decision you made or of having a physical body subject to deterioration and injury? In any event, what is your appropriate response, as a Christian, to those unpleasant circumstances?

FOR FURTHER STUDY

If you have access to the movie *The Hiding Place* about the World War II experiences of Corrie ten Boom, or to the book by the same name, view or read it this week. See whether this study gives you a better understanding of the experiences of Corrie and her family in that story.

If you don't have the book or movie, review these Bible verses to increase your understanding of the purposes of suffering:

- ❑ Romans 5:3–4
- ❑ 1 Corinthians 4:11–13
- ❑ 2 Timothy 3:12
- ❑ James 1:2–4

4

Responding to Your Enemies

LUKE 6:27–36; ROMANS 12:14–21

On January 8, 1956, five missionaries—Jim Elliot, Roger Youderian, Nate Saint, Pete Fleming, and Ed McCully—were killed by Auca Indians in the jungles of Ecuador. The five men had been attempting to establish contact with the virtually unknown, hostile tribe in order to present them with the gospel.

After the death of their husbands, the widows not only continued to pray for the Aucas, but most of them stayed in Ecuador with their young children to work as missionaries among the tribes. The result? Within three years most of the Aucas had been reached for Christ, and the Auca men who had killed the missionaries were playing with the slain men's children.

A tragic story with a happy ending. But *why* did those widows continue to love and pray for the Indians who had killed their husbands? If those who murder your family members aren't enemies, then the word *enemy* has no meaning.

In this study we will examine Christ's teaching about how we should respond to our enemies.

1. If you had been one of the wives of the slain missionaries, how do you think you would have responded? Why?

2. Read Luke 6:27–36. Why might those who treat their enemies as verses 27 and 28 suggest be labeled as "doormats" or "codependent"?

   How can we do what Christ commands without enabling the abusive behavior of our enemies?

3. In what ways can a friend or family member be an "enemy"?

4. Why do you think verses 29 and 30 are often rejected as impractical by practical people?

5. Does Jesus mean that if someone steals from us we should simply forget it (v. 30)? Explain.

6. Would following Christ's command in verse 30 mean that drug addicts or thieves could steal us blind, to their own detriment? Explain.

7. How would you express as a simple principle why Jesus tells us to love our enemies (vv. 32–36)?

8. Read Romans 12:14–21. In what specific ways can we "bless" those who persecute us (v. 14)?

9. In our status-conscious society, what tension might we feel with Paul's command, "Do not be proud, but be willing to associate with people of low position" (v. 16)?

Why might we feel proud toward those who persecute us, considering them "people of low position"?

10. Paul encourages us to "be careful to do what is right in the eyes of everybody" (v. 17). But traditional folk wisdom cautions us that "You can't please everybody." Can these two apparently contradictory pieces of advice be reconciled? Explain?

11. What are the practical implications of verse 18:

❏ in family life?

❏ at the workplace?

❏ in church life?

12. When you feel like taking revenge or getting even, how does it help you to know that: "'It is mine to avenge; I will repay,' says the Lord" (v. 19)?

13. What is the ultimate goal of responding to our enemies with prayer, love, and blessing, rather than hatred and cursing (vv. 20–21)?

MEMORY VERSES

"But I tell you who hear me: Love your enemies, do good to those who hate you, bless those who curse you, pray for those who mistreat you."

Luke 6:27–28

BETWEEN STUDIES

In your prayer times this week, instead of praying primarily for those you love (as most of us usually do), spend much of your time praying for an "enemy"—someone who is working against you.

If you're an antiabortion activist, for instance, try praying for a pro-choice activist or a NOW leader. And don't pray merely that your enemy will change his or her mind and begin to like you or to support your cause. Pray for your enemy's family, marriage, health, and spiritual life. At the end of the week, reexamine your feelings toward that person. Have they changed?

FOR FURTHER STUDY

For further insight into the lives of those missionaries martyred in Ecuador in 1956 and their families, read *Through Gates of Splendor* by Elisabeth Elliot (New York: Harper & Row, 1957) and *Unfolding Destinies* by Olive Fleming-Liefeld (Grand Rapids, Mich.: Zondervan Publishing House, 1991).

5

Fixing Your Eyes on Jesus

HEBREWS 12:1–12

> One night a man . . . dreamed he was walking along a beach with the Lord. Across the sky flashed scenes from his life. For each scene, he noticed two sets of footprints in the sand; one belonged to him, and the other to the Lord.

That, of course, is the beginning of a little story entitled "Footprints" that has appeared on posters and greeting cards for years. In it the man notices that during the "lowest and saddest" times in his life there was only one set of footprints. He asks the Lord why he abandoned him during those difficult times.

"My . . . child," the Lord replies, "during your times of trial and suffering, when you see only one set of footprints, it was then that I carried you."

Many of us have scoffed at that story as overused, trite, or corny. And yet there's a reason that it has proven so enduringly popular. Despite its sentimentalism, it conveys a profound truth: Jesus *does* help us through the difficult times in life. He will not abandon us. During times of opposition or rejection, he is at our side—or is, perhaps, carrying us.

1. What well-known historical or contemporary figures have been persecuted for what they believed or for the stand they took?

   In what ways can we benefit from their example?

2. Read Hebrews 12:1–12. The author imagines an athletic contest in a great amphitheater (vv. 1–3). What other details of the scene can you fill in?

3. The amphitheater is filled with those who have completed their race—the heroes of chapter 11. What do you think these "witnesses" (v. 1) would say to us as we run our race?

4. "Fix our eyes on Jesus" (v. 2) obviously doesn't refer to our physical sight. How, then, do we "fix our eyes on Jesus"?

5. Why should Jesus' example make our own sufferings any easier to bear or more meaningful?

6. Most of us aren't asked to shed blood as the price for resisting sin (v. 4). In what parts of the world are believers sometimes forced to shed blood for their beliefs?

In our culture, what are the most severe penalties we may be asked to pay?

7. Sometimes our suffering makes us feel that God does not love us. Why should we, in fact, feel just the opposite (vv. 5–8)?

8. We normally think of suffering and persecution as negative. Yet how can God use them in positive ways (vv. 9–11)?

9. If suffering is God's way of disciplining us, then does our suffering actually come from God? Explain.

10. Describe incidents from your past in which suffering or persecution produced "righteousness and peace" (v. 11) in your life.

11. How can our willingness—or unwillingness—to submit to God's discipline affect its results in our lives (v. 12)?

12. Ask God for the strength to endure whatever hardships you are facing and the grace to grow in the process.

MEMORY VERSES

Let us fix our eyes on Jesus, the author and perfecter of our faith, who for the joy set before him endured the cross, scorning its shame, and sat down at the right hand of the throne of God. Consider him who endured such opposition from sinful men, so that you will not grow weary and lose heart.

Hebrews 12:2–3

BETWEEN STUDIES

In the coming week, devise a system by which you can remind yourself to keep your eyes on Jesus during times of suffering. For example, you could pray whenever you see a difficult situation arising. Or you could find an appropriate verse (this week's memory verse, for instance) to recite whenever you feel your stress level rising. You could institute an end-of-day evaluation time (just before you prepare for bed, for instance) during which you think through the day's difficulties, pray about them, and consider how Jesus might have responded to those problems. Find a system that works best for you, and begin putting it into practice this week.

FOR FURTHER STUDY

Hebrews 12:3 encourages us to "consider him who endured such opposition from sinful men." Read the following passages that tell of the persecution and sufferings of Christ:

- ❑ Matthew 8:34; 11:16–19; 26:31–35, 38–45, 69–75; 27:24–50
- ❑ Mark 6:3–6
- ❑ Luke 4:28–29
- ❑ John 10:24–39

How did Jesus respond? What can we learn from his example?

6

Receiving Your Reward

MATTHEW 5:10–12; LUKE 6:22–23, 26

As part of my treatment for leukemia, I had to inject myself with Interferon three times a week for a year. My daughter Bethie, in first grade then, watched between her fingers one day as I injected my leg, and she asked, "How can you give your own self a shot? Doesn't it hurt?"

"It doesn't hurt much if I think about being well some day," I replied.

Like the football coach who endures the long months of hard work by putting a picture of the championship trophy in front of his desk, or the salesman who looks every night at the picture of his dream sailboat, I thought about the end result and ignored the periods of discomfort. And when the leukemia was under control and I was feeling healthy again, the pain I'd gone through to get there seemed insignificant.

Christ offers us the same hope to help us deal with suffering: Endure the unpleasantness, because the reward will be worth it.

1. When have you had a long and perhaps agonizing wait to receive something you really wanted?

2. Read Matthew 5:10–12. This is the only beatitude in which Jesus repeats his blessing and promise twice. Why do you think he emphasizes this beatitude?

3. One author remarked about verse 10, "Those who set their hearts on the kingdom cannot live in peace in this world."[1] Do you think he was correct? Why?

4. What is the importance of the words "because of righteousness" and "falsely" (vv. 10–11)?

5. Describe an incident in which you feel you were insulted, persecuted, or lied about because of your faith in Christ.

How did that experience make you feel?

6. When you think of your reward in heaven—that which should make you "rejoice and be glad"—what images come to mind?

7. When people insult you or persecute you because of Christ, how does it help to know that "great is your reward in heaven" (v. 12)?

8. Read Luke 6:22–23, and 26. What additional kinds of persecution does Luke's account add to the list (v. 22)?

9. Jesus warns us to beware when everyone speaks well of us (v. 26). Why is the praise and approval of others such a powerful motivation?

10. In what situations might the praise of others be a negative thing?

11. Throughout the beatitudes Jesus stands the world's values on their head. How should this final beatitude affect our views of success and failure?

MEMORY VERSES

Blessed are you when people insult you, persecute you and falsely say all kinds of evil against you because of me. Rejoice and be glad, because great is your reward in heaven.

Matthew 5:11–12

BETWEEN STUDIES

Write a letter to God. List for him some of the things you fear or that cause you pain. Then write a description of eternal blessings he has planned for you in heaven. Close by explaining to God just how significant those fears and pains you began the letter with really are in comparison with all God has done and will do. Ask for his help in keeping a proper perspective.

FOR FURTHER STUDY

Read Romans 8:12–39. What does this wonderful passage teach us about the meaning of our present persecutions and sufferings, and about the "joy" we will experience because of them?

Examine the following passages also:

- ❑ 2 Corinthians 1:3–5; 4:16–17
- ❑ 2 Timothy 2:11–13
- ❑ 1 Peter 4:12–16

What light do they shed on the Romans 8 passage?

Note

1. H. N. Ridderbos, *Matthew: Bible Student's Commentary* (Grand Rapids, Mich.: Zondervan Publishing House, 1987), p. 92.

Leader's Notes

Leading a Bible discussion—especially for the first time—can make you feel both nervous and excited. If you are nervous, realize that you are in good company. Many biblical leaders, such as Moses, Joshua, and the apostle Paul, felt nervous and inadequate to lead others (see, for example, 1 Corinthians 2:3). Yet God's grace was sufficient for them, just as it will be for you.

Some excitement is also natural. Your leadership is a gift to the others in the group. Keep in mind, however, that other group members also share responsibility for the group. Your role is simply to stimulate discussion by asking questions and encouraging people to respond. The suggestions listed below can help you to be an effective leader.

PREPARING TO LEAD

1. Ask God to help you understand and apply the passage to your own life. Unless that happens, you will not be prepared to lead others.

2. Carefully work through each question in the study guide. Meditate and reflect on the passage as you formulate your answers.

3. Familiarize yourself with the leader's notes for the study. These will help you understand the purpose of the study

and will provide valuable information about the questions in the study.

4. Pray for the various members of the group. Ask God to use these studies to make you better disciples of Jesus Christ.

5. Before the first meeting, make sure each person has a study guide. Encourage them to prepare beforehand for each study.

LEADING THE STUDY

1. Begin the study on time. If people realize that the study begins on schedule, they will work harder to arrive on time.

2. At the beginning of your first time together, explain that these studies are designed to be discussions, not lectures. Encourage everyone to participate, but realize that some may be hesitant to speak during the first few sessions.

3. Read the introductory paragraph at the beginning of the discussion. This will orient the group to the passage being studied.

4. Read the passage aloud. You may choose to do this yourself, or you might ask for volunteers.

5. The questions in the guide are designed to be used just as they are written. If you wish, you may simply read each one aloud to the group. Or you may prefer to express them in your own words. Unnecessary rewording of the questions, however, is not recommended.

6. Don't be afraid of silence. People in the group may need time to think before responding.

7. Avoid answering your own questions. If necessary, rephrase a question until it is clearly understood. Even an eager group will quickly become passive and silent if they think the leader will do most of the talking.

8. Encourage more than one answer to each question. Ask, "What do the rest of you think?" or "Anyone else?" until several people have had a chance to respond.

9. Try to be affirming whenever possible. Let people know you appreciate their insights into the passage.

10. Never reject an answer. If it is clearly wrong, ask, "Which verse led you to that conclusion?" Or let the group handle the problem by asking them what they think about the question.

11. Avoid going off on tangents. If people wander off course, gently bring them back to the passage being considered.

12. Conclude your time together with conversational prayer. Ask God to help you apply those things that you learned in the study.

13. End on time. This will be easier if you control the pace of the discussion by not spending too much time on some questions or too little on others.

Many more suggestions and helps are found in the book *Leading Bible Discussions* (InterVarsity Press). Reading it would be well worth your time.

STUDY 1
Standing Strong
DANIEL 3:8–27; JOB 1

Purpose: To observe how we can stand strong in the face of persecution and wait patiently in the midst of suffering.

Question 1 Every study begins with an "approach question," which is discussed *before* reading the passage. An approach question is designed to do three things.

First, it helps to break the ice. Because an approach question doesn't require any knowledge of the passage or any special preparation, it can get people talking and can help them to warm up to each other.

Second, an approach question can motivate people to study the passage at hand. At the beginning of the study, people in the group aren't necessarily ready to jump into the world of the Bible. Their minds may be on other things (their kids, a problem at work, an upcoming meeting) that have nothing to do with the study. An approach question can capture their interest and draw them into the discussion by raising important issues related to the study. The question becomes a bridge between their personal lives and the answers found in Scripture.

Third, a good approach question can reveal where people's thoughts or feelings need to be transformed by Scripture. That is why it is important to ask the approach question *before* reading the passage. The passage might inhibit the spontaneous, honest answers people might have given, because they feel compelled to give biblical answers. The approach question allows them to compare their personal thoughts and feelings with what they later discover in Scripture.

Question 2 The astrologers were most likely jealous of the three Jews' success in Nebuchadnezzar's kingdom. The king had placed the Jews "over the affairs of the province of Babylon" (v. 12). This was also the reason that officials in Nebuchadnezzar's court sought charges against Daniel in Daniel 6:1–5. The astrologers may also have been angry that the Jews would not worship the cultic gods the astrologers revered (v. 12).

Question 3 They seem confident, though they may in fact have been terrified. They speak boldly and clearly—even heroically, considering that they don't know whether God will rescue them from the furnace or allow them to be martyred for his glory.

Part of the reason for their boldness is hinted at in their first statement to Nebuchadnezzar: "'O Nebuchadnezzar,' the three said, 'we do not need to defend ourselves before you in this matter.' . . . The Aramaic word order of verse 16 places an emphasis on the pronoun 'we,' implying that it is the Lord himself who will deal with this king who thinks he is sovereign on earth" (Gleason L. Archer, Jr., *Daniel*, The Expositor's Bible Commentary [Grand Rapids, Mich.: Zondervan Publishing House, 1985], p. 54).

Question 4 Despite their boldness, their reply differs from that of a warrior because they are not combative. They have, in fact, complied with the king's commands as far as they were able, and they have not been arrogant or obnoxious in their refusal to violate their consciences. Even so, their reply differs from that of the diplomat because they leave no room for compromise. They take their stand firmly and accept the inevitability of a violent response. And in that, they differ greatly from the coward, who would have violated his conscience rather than face painful death.

Question 5 The meaning would have been quite different. God, in his sovereignty, chose to rescue the three Jews, thereby making this story an example to his people as well as to their enemies that God is able and willing to preserve his people in persecution, by supernatural intervention if need be. Had he allowed Shadrach, Meshach, and Abednego to be martyred, God would still have been glorified—but the story would have been less about his ability to preserve his people and more about their devotion and bravery.

Question 9 Satan scoffs at Job's godliness, claiming that his is a mercenary devotion. Job serves God, Satan claims, only because God protects and prospers him. "Satan's words are too true of many. Take away their prosperity and you take away their religion" (Jamieson, Fausset, and Brown, *Commentary on the Whole Bible*, p. 364).

Question 13 There's quite a contrast between the three Jews standing valiantly before Nebuchadnezzar and Job, head shaved, clothes ripped, prostrate in the dirt. Whereas

Shadrach, Meshach, and Abednego were bold, confident, even heroic. Job is broken, grief-stricken, hopeless ("naked I will depart")—but still worshipful. Though their reactions were very different, all four men responded appropriately and sinlessly to their persecution (see Job 1:22). Job's reply is a reply of strength because he retains both his integrity and his sense of God's sovereignty; he worships.

Question 14 We see that there can be more than one model for dealing with persecution and hardship appropriately. We benefit from their examples of integrity, boldness, fearlessness, stubborn faith in God, and willingness to accept any loss or even death in God's sovereign will. And we can take heart in the fact that, even in their darkest hour, God did not desert any of these people. He saw them through their persecution, and he restored them to even greater heights afterward.

STUDY 2
Obeying God Rather than Man
ACTS 5:12–42

Purpose: To learn from the apostles why we must be willing to obey God at all costs—even if we are forbidden by law and threatened with imprisonment.

Question 2 The Sanhedrin and the high priest were jealous that the crowds were more devoted and protective of the apostles than of their Jewish religious leaders. A second reason for their jealousy, one they would never have discussed among themselves, might have been that they were jealous of the apostles' power. Luke mentions, "And all of them were healed" (v. 16). The religious leaders knew that they did not have the power to stand out in the temple courts and heal the sick and cast out evil spirits.

Question 5 They may, of course, have been angry that the apostles had scorned the high priest's authority and disobeyed his direct orders not to teach in the name of Christ. They may have been angry that the apostles had escaped from prison. And, as Donald Grey Barnhouse points out, "Isn't it strange that the first-century ministerial union should be annoyed and indignant that people were getting saved, healed, and blessed. But that's frequently the case. Entrenched religion wants things done in an entrenched way where the men who are running the show can continue to control things. It was inevitable that the apostles would face further persecution. In the eyes of the religious leaders they were troublemakers, stirring up the status quo" (*Acts: An Expositional Commentary* [Grand Rapids, Mich.: Zondervan Publishing House, 1979], pp. 54–55).

But it's also very likely that they were fearful. "You . . . are determined to make us guilty of this man's blood," they say in verse 28. And yet at Christ's crucifixion, which they engineered, they cried along with the people, "Let his blood be on us and on our children!" (Matt. 27:25). Obviously, in the months since the crucifixion, they had become uneasy about being blamed for his death. They feared some reprisal, some blame. Their guilty consciences prodded them to act in anger toward the apostles. Eliminating the apostles would eliminate the reminders of their own guilt.

Christians are persecuted for similar reasons today. Godless regimes persecute Christians because they fear the loyalty and devotion Christians have to their leaders, to Christ, and to justice. They (rightly) perceive Christianity as a threat. Individuals sometimes persecute Christians because it provides some relief from their own guilty consciences.

Questions 7–8 The angel of the Lord who released them from prison also gave them explicit instructions, which they obeyed. There was no need for them to puzzle over what God wanted them to do next.

Though we may not have angels delivering God's instructions to us, we have Scripture, which often tells us very clearly what to do in particular circumstances. We have prayer, which God answers. We have the wise counsel of our elders, and we have the witness of the Holy Spirit within us, speaking through our consciences.

Question 9 God did not protect Job from harm. Although he ultimately restored Job's wealth, he did not restore life to his dead children. God did not protect Stephen from harm in Acts 7. And tradition tells us that the apostles died as martyrs.

So many missionaries died in Africa in the nineteenth century that it became known as the "White Man's Graveyard." In later studies in this guide, we'll examine the appropriate Christian response to the knowledge that we might not be able to escape suffering for God's sake, and what reassurances God gives us about that possibility.

Question 11 All of us, children and adults, sometimes face pressure from our friends and acquaintances to do what we know is wrong. We can resist that pressure and choose to obey God, even though we may be abandoned by those friends. Many Christians around the world are forced to choose between God and the laws of their country, from those in China who attend unlawful Christian worship services to those in America who picket abortion clinics. And society itself gives us patterns and values—looking out for number one, upward mobility, conspicuous consumption, racism, irresponsible sensuality, substance abuse—that we as responsible Christians must refuse if we are to obey God.

STUDY 3
Suffering as a Christian
1 PETER 1:6–7; 2:19–23; 4:12–19

Purpose: To examine the inevitability of suffering in the life of the Christian, and to explore the sometimes beneficial effects of that suffering.

Question 1 If your group has a hard time thinking of some of the "less practical" aspects of Christianity, ask them to think of some of the difficult commands in the Sermon on the Mount: turning the other cheek, lending to those who can't repay, loving their enemies, and so on. Or of some of the paradoxes of Christianity, such as: "Whoever finds his life will lose it, and whoever loses his life for my sake will find it" (Matt. 10:39). Or such self-sacrificial commands as: "Do nothing out of selfish ambition or vain conceit, but in humility consider others better than yourselves" (Phil. 2:3).

Question 2 Peter seems to clarify in other verses in his first epistle that trials and suffering can be expected throughout our life on earth, that they have a positive purpose, and that God "will himself restore you and make you strong, firm and steadfast" in eternity (1 Pet. 5:10; see also 4:12–13).

Questions 4–5 The purpose of these questions is to bring home the difficulty of behaving as this passage encourages us to. Your group members will probably have no trouble remembering a time they were punished justly. Those who can remember a time when they were punished unjustly will probably remember and may still feel a sense of outrage. And yet bearing that injustice patiently is exactly what is spoken of in verse 20 as "commendable before God."

In his *Expository Dictionary of Bible Words*, Larry Richards suggests why this is so: "To produce its greatest benefits, suffering is not to be a consequence of our own sinful choices. . . . Moreover, suffering should be viewed as fellowship (*koinonia*, "participation"). Jesus suffered for his commitment to doing the will of God. A similar commitment on our part leads to a uniquely "Christian" suffering, which is linked with the completion of Jesus' mission on earth and which is in fact an aspect of fellowship (a close relationship) with our Lord (e.g., 1 Pe 4:1, 13; Php 3:10). Thus, truly Christian suffering is also purposive: it is for the sake of Jesus, his kingdom, and his righteousness (e.g., Ac 9:16; Php 1:29; 2 Th 1:5; 1 Pe 2:19; 3:14; 4:14, 16, 19)" (Grand Rapids, Mich.: Zondervan Publishing House, 1985, p. 476).

Question 6 If your group has a hard time understanding this reference, read through verses 21–23 carefully, pointing out that just as Jesus did not retaliate when he was made to suffer, instead entrusting himself to God as an act of faith, so we too can express our faith in God by suffering patiently, trusting in God to act on our behalf.

Question 7 It's likely that some of your group members may have raised doubts about the practicality of suffering injustice patiently. Common sense tells us to stand up for ourselves if we're unjustly punished or accused, and to protect ourselves. The purpose of this question is to partially answer those objections by pointing out that Jesus' friends probably told him the same thing, as we would have if we had been there. Yet the purpose of his suffering is now clear to us. Indeed, the fate of all mankind hung on his acting just as he did. Sometimes Christians are called to act "unreasonably" (at least from the world's point of view).

Question 8 If your group members don't seem to understand the passage, read Psalm 9:4, Romans 12:19–21, and Luke 23:46 for other instances of entrusting ourselves to God, who judges justly.

"Leave your case in His hands, not desiring to make Him executioner of your revenge, but rather praying for enemies. God's *righteous judgment* gives tranquility and consolation to the oppressed" (Jamieson, Fausset, and Brown, *Commentary on the Whole Bible,* p. 1474). Encourage your group to examine the implications of this principle in such matters as disagreements with friends or family members, business ethics, use of the courts, traffic etiquette, and so on.

Question 10 According to Jamieson, Fausset, and Brown's *Commentary on the Whole Bible*, we participate in Christ's sufferings when we are "willingly for His sake suffering as He suffered" (p. 1480). The key word there may be *willingly*— not struggling against our persecution, but rather submitting to it.

Matthew Henry points out that we participate with Christ in another way—*he* participates with us in our sufferings. When we suffer, he suffers with us (*Commentary in One Volume* [Grand Rapids, Mich.: Zondervan Publishing House, 1961], p. 1947).

Question 12 Through our hardship, we can provide "praise, glory and honor when Jesus Christ is revealed" (1:7), and we ourselves will be overjoyed at that time (4:13). And when we are reproached and reviled and insulted, we are "blessed, for the Spirit of glory and of God rests on [us]" (4:14).

Question 13 We may expect to suffer, and we may expect that suffering will have many purposes and benefits. We are to greatly rejoice in those sufferings.

To be commendable before God, our suffering should not be a result of our own wrongs; rather, it should be for doing good and should be borne patiently, as Christ suffered.

Christians endure suffering because we entrust ourselves to God, who judges justly. Christians are not ashamed to suffer according to God's will.

STUDY 4
Responding to Your Enemies
LUKE 6:27–36; ROMANS 12:14–21

Purpose: To examine some of the ways Scripture encourages us to respond to our enemies, and to investigate why we are to act in those ways.

Question 2 Your group may have varied responses to this question, some arguing that it's not possible to respond as these verses suggest without enabling abusive behavior. Yet it must be possible, for these verses cannot be untrue.

It is important to note that, as Walter W. Wessel points out, "The word 'love' (*agape* in the noun form) must be understood in its classic Christian sense of having a genuine concern for someone irrespective of his or her attractiveness or of the likelihood of any reciprocation in kind" (*Luke,* The Expositor's Bible Commentary [Grand Rapids, Mich.: Zondervan Publishing House, 1984], p. 893). In other words, Christ was not speaking merely of the love we feel for those with whom we are in a romantic or family relationship, but rather of the God-given love we are to feel for *all* people.

Agape love is always strong, never weak. It is weakness to allow yourself to be abused, to allow the one you love to harm himself or herself by falling into an abusive behavior pattern. Therefore, that type of behavior is not advocated by this passage. *Agape* love is characterized by self-control, not domination by others.

Questions 5–6 Walter W. Wessel writes that "Jesus is not advocating the suspension of normal civil judicial procedures. If pagan governments abandoned the protection of civil rights, the result would be an unbiblical anarchy (Rom. 13:4).

. . . The teaching of the passage as a whole relates not so much to passivity in the face of evil as to concern for the other person. Inevitably, as ancient Greek philosophers recognized, to refrain from doing evil often means suffering evil. . . .

The same spirit is expressed in v. 30, where the practical application of this hyperbolic command would be to refuse to demand that which would genuinely be to the good of the other person, even at our expense" (Luke, p. 893).

Question 7 We are to strive to be like Jesus. We should love our enemies because God loves those who are ungrateful and wicked and because Jesus loved and asked forgiveness for those who killed him.

Question 9 Make sure that your discussion brings out to everyone in your group that our society pressures us to associate with the "right" people and to avoid the "wrong" people.

Our social standing often depends on it—and not just in the schoolyard.

We often classify those who persecute us in any way as the "wrong" people, outside the boundary of God's provision and protection. We feel no responsibility to love them.

If your group has trouble with the second part of this question, look again at the introduction to this study and discuss whether the missionaries' widows would not have been "within their rights" to hate and reject those who murdered their husbands, and what the consequences of that choice might have been.

Question 10 Despite our attempts to "do what is right in the eyes of everybody," many will misunderstand and hate and persecute us anyway. But God never makes us responsible for the choices of others. It is simply our responsibility to obey him and try to "live in harmony with one another" (v. 16). If others choose not to respond positively to us, our attempt was no less scriptural.

Question 11 Encourage your group to be specific and practical in their responses to this question. Ask them to think about particular relationships—with spouse, children, boss, coworkers, pastor, neighbors, and so on—and particular situations, such as marital disagreements, disciplining children, uncooperative coworkers, church committees, or friction at church.

Question 13 Everett F. Harrison writes that "in this context, 'to be overcome by evil' means to give in to the temptation to meet evil with evil, to retaliate. To overcome evil with good has been illustrated in v. 20. Many other illustrations could be given, such as David's sparing the life of Saul, who was pursuing him to snuff out his life. When Saul realized that David had spared his life, he said, 'You have repaid me good, whereas I have repaid you evil' (1 Sam 24:17 RSV). The world's philosophy leads men to expect retaliation when they have wronged another. To receive kindness, to see love when it seems uncalled for, can melt the hardest heart" (*Romans,* The Expositor's Bible Commentary [Grand Rapids, Mich.: Zondervan Publishing House, 1976], p. 135).

STUDY 5
Fixing Your Eyes on Jesus
HEBREWS 12:1–12

Purpose: To consider why we should focus on Jesus Christ in the midst of our suffering. To realize that suffering can be a form of God's loving discipline.

Question 1 Many of the people your group members might name—Martin Luther King, Jr., Randall Terry of Operation Rescue, Nelson Mandela, and so on—will be controversial. Don't let your group's discussion of these individuals degenerate into a debate over the political or spiritual beliefs of the people you identify. The purpose of the question is simply to identify individuals who suffered for their beliefs, regardless of the rightness or wrongness of those beliefs.

Question 4 The responses to this question should be very practical. We fix our eyes on Jesus when we pray, when we speak of him to each other, when we sing gospel songs to ourselves in the car on the way to work, when we have our daily devotional time, when we habitually bring his example to mind every time we encounter opposition, and so on. The ideas your group brainstorms should be things they can put into practice in their daily lives.

Question 5 Leon Morris writes that "Suffering comes to all; it is part of life, but it is not easy to bear. Yet it is not quite so bad when it can be seen as meaningful. The author has just pointed out that Christ endured his suffering on the cross on account of the joy set before him. His suffering had meaning. So for Christians all suffering is transformed because of the Cross. We serve a Savior who suffered, and we know he will not lead us into meaningless suffering. The writer points to the importance of discipline and proceeds to show that for Christians suffering is rightly understood only when seen as God's fatherly discipline, correcting and directing us. Suffering is evidence, not that God does not love us, but that he does. Believers are sons and are treated as sons" (*Hebrews,* The Expositor's Bible Commentary [Grand Rapids, Mich.: Zondervan, 1981], p. 136).

Matthew Henry also tells us that "We must look unto him; we must set him continually before us as our example. We must consider him, meditate much upon him. . . .

The advantage we shall reap by thus doing: it will be a means to prevent our weariness and fainting (v. 3). There is a proneness in the best to grow weary and to faint under their trials and afflictions. The best way to prevent this is to look unto Jesus. Faith and meditation will fetch in fresh supplies of strength, comfort and courage" (*Commentary in One Volume,* p. 1926).

Question 6 Group members who don't keep up on current events may not be able to identify areas of the globe where Christians are currently being physically persecuted (China, for instance, as well as parts of Africa and the Muslim Middle East). Remind them of such historical atrocities as the Roman persecution of Christians by such means as crucifixion and lions, and the Soviet Union's attempts to eradicate the church by force. Even in our country, Christians who speak out for their beliefs may be passed over for promotion, lose their jobs or, like Anita Bryant when she spoke out against homosexuality, be subjected to smear campaigns in the media. We may lose friends, be shunned by society, and could even be physically injured for our beliefs if those who oppose us hate us enough.

Question 8 To the extent that the suffering and persecution we encounter are also God's discipline, they are positive as well as negative. And discipline is not always punishment. A coach subjects his athletes to difficult workouts to discipline their bodies, not as punishment for something they've done wrong. Likewise, God sometimes allows us to experience difficulties and persecutions to toughen and strengthen us. That analogy is strengthened by the fact that, throughout this passage, the author uses athletics as a metaphor for the Christian life.

Matthew Henry also comments that "those afflictions which may be truly persecution as far as men are concerned in them are fatherly rebukes and chastisements as far as God is concerned in them. Men persecute them because they are religious; God chastises them because they are not more so" (*Commentary in One Volume*, p. 1927).

Question 9 The theological issues suggested by this question are too great to cover in a short session, but they're unnecessary to understanding the crucial principle here—that God never induces people to sin, and therefore those people who unjustly persecute us do so of their own free will, not because they have been "put up to it" by God as a way of disciplining us. Even so, God expects us to use these situations as opportunities to grow spiritually. Other forms of adversity-as-discipline, such as sickness and disappointment, may indeed come directly from God.

Question 10 Group members may need a few minutes to think of appropriate responses to this question, so be prepared to start with examples from your own life.

STUDY 6
Receiving Your Reward
MATTHEW 5:10–12; LUKE 6:22–23, 26

Purpose: To investigate those rewards that Jesus assures us will be ours if we endure persecution.

Question 3 That sentence comes from H. N. Ridderbos's commentary on Matthew. He observes further that "the fate that awaits Jesus' disciples because of their relationship to Him is contempt, persecution, and slander. Driven by hate, people will utter all kinds of evil against them. . . .

If they accept this fate for Jesus' sake, they are blessed. Indeed they can rejoice greatly, since their misfortune on earth will prove that they are among those who have a great reward in heaven.

Jesus, in such passages as John 15:18–20, gave his disciples a clear promise that they would be persecuted. Truly, the more we follow Christ's example, the less peace we will experience in our relationships with those around us. But God also promises us a 'peace . . . which transcends all understanding' (Phil. 4:7), even in the midst of persecution" (*Matthew*, p. 93).

Question 4 The context of the passages in both Luke and Matthew make it clear that we are blessed when we are persecuted (1) because of righteousness and (2) falsely. Especially in these days when so many prominent Christians have fallen into public sin and disgrace, it should be easy for us to discern between persecution for Christ's sake and persecution because of sin.

If we *deserve* the insults and the ill treatment and punishment, we can't expect spiritual credit for enduring it. It is just payment for our foolish or sinful acts. (See also 1 Peter 2:20; 3:15–17; 4:15.)

Question 10 The world hates us because we follow Christ and therefore have a value system entirely alien to those who are persecuting us. The reverse is also true: If the world *doesn't* hate us, then perhaps our value system isn't as different as it's supposed to be. Micah 2:11 and John 15:19 make this principle clear. Anytime we take a stand for our Christian values and are met with acceptance and applause by the world at large, we'd better reexamine our values to make sure we've spoken correctly.

Notes